AFFIRM YOUR GREATNESS

HARNESSING THE POWER OF POSITIVE AFFIRMATIONS

DENNIS M. MBOGORI

Affirm Your Greatness

Harnessing the Power of Positive Affirmations

by
Dennis M.Mbogori

Copyright ©2024 by Dennis M. Mbogori
All rights reserved. No part of this book may be reproduced, scanned,
or distributed in any printed or electronic form without permission.
Second Edition: January 2025
Printed in the United States of America
ISBN: **9798339012252**

To My Wife Sarah,
Thanks for Seeing and Speaking Greatness
Into Me.

Dennis M. Mbogori

Table of Contents

Understanding Affirmations: What They Are and How They Work   1
   What Are Affirmations?   1
   The Science Behind Affirmations   1
   How Affirmations Work   2
   Crafting Effective Affirmations   3
   Examples of Affirmations and Their Implementation   4
     Emma's Journey to Confidence: Unleashing the Power of Positive Affirmations   6

The Science Behind Positive Affirmations   11
   The Psychological Basis   11
   The Neurological Perspective   12
   The Role of Self-Affirmation Theory   12
   Scientific Studies and Evidence   13
   Practical Examples of Positive Affirmations   13
     John's Transformation to Better Health: Unleashing the Power of Positive Affirmations   15

Crafting Your Powerful Affirmations   20
   Understanding the Components of Effective Affirmations   20
   Steps to Craft Your Affirmations   22
   Examples of Powerful Affirmations   24
   Personalizing Your Affirmations   25
   Incorporating Affirmations into Your Daily Routine   25
     Emily's Journey to Financial Abundance: Unleashing the Power of Positive Affirmations   27

Daily Practices to Integrate Affirmations into Your Life   32
   Morning Rituals   32
   Throughout the Day   33
   Evening Practices   34
   Integrating Affirmations into Activities   35

Visualization Techniques	36
Affirmations in Meditation	37
Affirming Love: Mark's Journey to Connection	39
Overcoming Negative Self-Talk	**44**
Understanding Negative Self-Talk	44
Identifying Negative Self-Talk	45
Challenging Negative Self-Talk	46
Replacing Negative Self-Talk with Positive Affirmations	46
Examples of Transforming Negative Self-Talk	48
Daily Practices to Overcome Negative Self-Talk	49
Liam: The Athlete's Triumph	51
Affirmations for Personal Growth and Self-Love	**54**
The Importance of Personal Growth and Self-Love	54
Crafting Affirmations for Personal Growth	55
Examples of Affirmations for Personal Growth	56
Crafting Affirmations for Self-Love	57
Examples of Affirmations for Self-Love	57
Integrating Affirmations into Your Daily Life	58
Sarah: The Student's Academic Breakthrough	61
Using Affirmations to Achieve Career Success	**64**
The Power of Positive Affirmations in Your Career	64
Crafting Effective Career Affirmations	66
Examples of Career Success Affirmations	67
Incorporating Affirmations into Your Daily Routine	69
Mark: The Artist's Creative Breakthrough	71
Health and Wellness: Affirmations for a Balanced Life	**74**
The Role of Affirmations in Health and Wellness	74
Crafting Effective Health and Wellness Affirmations	75
Examples of Health and Wellness Affirmations	76
Incorporating Affirmations into Your Daily Routine	78
Sandra: The Entrepreneur's Success	80
Financial Abundance: Manifesting Wealth through Positive Thoughts	**83**
The Power of Positive Affirmations in Financial Abundance	83

Crafting Effective Financial Abundance Affirmations   85
Examples of Financial Abundance Affirmations   86
Incorporating Affirmations into Your Daily Routine   88
    Larry: The Overcomer of Social Anxiety   90
Building Meaningful Relationships with Affirmations   93
The Role of Affirmations in Building Relationships   93
Crafting Effective Relationship Affirmations   94
Examples of Relationship Affirmations   95
Incorporating Affirmations into Your Daily Routine   97
    Maya: The Seeker of Inner Peace   99
How to Create Your Own Success Story   102
Epilogue: The Tapestry of Transformation   104
Conclusion: Embracing a Life of Positivity and Empowerment   108
The Journey of Self-Discovery   108
The Power of Consistency   109
Embracing a Positive Mindset   110
Taking Action   110
Your Path to Empowerment   111
More Resources   113

Affirm Your Greatness

Dennis M. Mbogori

A Note From The Author: Affirmations Work!

You may say to me as a man of faith, hey Dennis, Positive Affirmations are a bunch of psychological *mambo jumbo* or some new age fluff!

However, the Holy Scriptures are full of examples of Affirmations and consequences of low self-perception. For instance, God the creator introduced Himself to Moses, the deliverer, and prophet, as "I AM WHO I AM" *(Exodus 3:14 New Living Translation)*

On the opposing end of the spectrum, the Israelites whom Moses was sent to deliver from slavery saw themselves as Grasshoppers when it was time to conquer the promised land; instead, they backed down and took another 40 years in the wilderness. *(Numbers 13:33 New King James Version)*

One of the most quoted passages that can be used as a Positive Affirmation is: "For I can do everything through Christ, who gives me strength." *(Philippians 4:13 New Living Translation)*

When viewing or using Holy Scripture, be cautious and do so in the passage's context.

In the following pages, may you be encouraged and equipped as you learn how to use and apply positive affirmations.

This updated edition includes detailed stories and case studies at the end of each chapter, enhancing your understanding of the inner workings of personalized positive affirmations.

Enjoy your journey through *Affirm Your Greatness: Harnessing The Power of Positive Affirmations*.

See You on The Other Side,

Dennis M. Mbogori

Author, Affirm Your Greatness: Harnessing The Power of Positive Affirmations.

Dennis M. Mbogori

Introduction: The Journey to Self-Discovery

Welcome to a transformative journey that will unlock the hidden potential within you. Positive affirmations are a beacon of hope and empowerment in a world of challenges and uncertainties. This book, *"Affirm Your Greatness: Harnessing the Power of Positive Affirmations,"* is your guide to discovering positive thoughts and words' profound impact on your life.

Imagine waking up daily with purpose, confidence, and unwavering belief in your abilities. Picture yourself easily overcoming obstacles, achieving your goals, and living a life filled with joy and fulfillment. This is not just a dream—it's a reality you can create through positive affirmations.

In the following pages, you will learn what affirmations are, how they work, and why they are so powerful. You will discover the science behind this practice and how it can rewire your brain for success. We will guide you through crafting your affirmations, integrating them into your daily routine, and using them to overcome negative self-talk.

Whether you seek personal growth, career success, better health, financial abundance, or meaningful relationships, this book will provide the necessary tools and inspiration. Real-life success stories will illustrate the transformative power of affirmations, showing you that change is possible and within your reach.

So, take a deep breath, open your mind, and get ready to embark on a journey of self-discovery and empowerment. It's time to affirm your greatness and create the life you've always dreamed of.

Chapter 1

UNDERSTANDING AFFIRMATIONS: WHAT THEY ARE AND HOW THEY WORK

WHAT ARE AFFIRMATIONS?

Affirmations are positive statements you repeat to yourself to challenge and overcome self-sabotaging and negative thoughts. When you say or think about them, they can help you visualize and believe in the positive changes you aim for in your life. Affirmations are a powerful tool for personal development, helping to reprogram your subconscious mind and encourage a more positive outlook.

THE SCIENCE BEHIND AFFIRMATIONS

Psychological and neuroscientific research supports the effectiveness of affirmations. When you repeat a positive affirmation, you train your brain to think differently. This process is known as *neuroplasticity*, the brain's ability to reorganize itself by forming new neural connections. By consistently practicing affirmations, you can create new pathways in your brain that support positive thinking and behavior.

How Affirmations Work

Affirmations work by:

1. **Reinforcing Positive Beliefs**: By repeating positive statements, you reinforce the belief in your abilities and potential.
2. **Reducing Stress**: Positive affirmations can help reduce stress by promoting a calm and focused mindset.
3. **Boosting Confidence**: Regular use of affirmations can boost your self-esteem and confidence.
4. **Encouraging Positive Actions**: Affirmations can motivate you to act positively towards your goals.

CRAFTING EFFECTIVE AFFIRMATIONS

To create powerful affirmations, follow these guidelines:

1. **Be Positive**: Focus on what you want, not what you don't want. For example, instead of saying, *"I am not stressed,"* say, *"I am calm and relaxed."*
2. **Be Present**: Phrase your affirmations in the present tense as if they are already happening. For example, *"I am successful"* instead of *"I will be successful."*
3. **Be Specific**: Make your affirmations specific to your goals and desires. For example, *"I am confident in my ability to speak in public"* instead of *"I am confident."*
4. **Be Personal**: Use "I" statements to make your affirmations personal and relevant to you.

Examples of Affirmations and Their Implementation

Here are some examples of affirmations and how you can implement them in your daily life:

1. **Affirmation for Self-Love**: *"I am worthy of love and respect."*
   - **Implementation**: Repeat this affirmation every morning while looking at yourself in the mirror. Write it down in your journal and reflect on it before going to bed.

2. **Affirmation for Career Success**: *"I can achieve great success in my career."*
   - **Implementation**: Say this affirmation before starting your workday. Visualize yourself achieving your career goals and take actionable steps towards them.

3. **Affirmation for Health and Wellness**: *"I am healthy, strong, and energetic."*
   - **Implementation**: Use this affirmation during your exercise routine or when preparing healthy meals. Incorporate it

into your meditation or mindfulness practice.

4. **Affirmation for Financial Abundance:** *"I attract wealth and abundance into my life."*
   - **Implementation:** Repeat this affirmation while reviewing your financial goals. Visualize yourself achieving economic stability and abundance.

5. **Affirmation for Building Relationships:** *"Loving and supportive people surround me."*
   - **Implementation:** Say this affirmation before social events or interactions. Focus on building meaningful connections and expressing gratitude for your relationships.

By integrating these affirmations into your daily routine, you can see positive changes in your mindset and overall well-being. Remember, consistency is key. The more you practice, the more effective your affirmations will become.

Emma's Journey to Confidence: Unleashing the Power of Positive Affirmations

Emma, a talented graphic designer, lived a life plagued by self-doubt and anxiety. Despite her skills, she often felt inadequate, plagued by limiting beliefs like *"I'm not good enough"* and *"I'm afraid to fail."* This constant self-criticism hindered her professional growth and impacted her relationships.

One day, her friend Sarah, a personal development coach, noticed Emma's struggles. Sarah suggested incorporating daily affirmations into her routine. Emma was initially skeptical. How could simply repeating positive statements make any real difference?

Sarah explained, "Affirmations work by rewiring your subconscious mind. By consistently telling yourself positive things, you start to believe them on a deeper level." Intrigued, Emma decided to give it a try.

Every morning, she stood in front of the mirror and repeated affirmations like, *"I am a talented and confident designer."* She replaced negative self-talk with empowering statements, such as: *"I am worthy of success and recognition."* She personalized her affirmations, acknowledging her unique strengths and talents.

Initially, it felt awkward and unnatural, but Emma persisted. She repeated her affirmations with conviction, gradually infusing them with emotion and visualizing herself achieving her goals. She even wrote her affirmations on sticky notes and placed them around her workspace, creating constant reminders of her commitment to self-improvement.

Emma began to notice subtle shifts in her mindset. She felt more confident during client meetings, expressing her ideas with greater clarity and conviction. She started taking on more challenging projects, enthusiastically embracing new creative endeavors. Her colleagues noticed the change, praising her for her newfound confidence and creativity.

Emma was invited to present her work at a prestigious design conference one day. In the past, such an opportunity would have paralyzed her with fear. However, this time, she felt calm and assured. Her affirmations had instilled a deep sense of self-belief. She delivered her presentation with poise and confidence, receiving a standing ovation from the audience.

Emma realized that affirmations had transformed her life. They had helped her overcome her self-doubt, unlock her true potential, and achieve success beyond her initial expectations. She continued to use affirmations as a powerful tool for personal and professional growth, embracing them as an integral part of her daily routine.

Emma's story inspires, demonstrating the transformative power of positive thinking. By:

- Identifying and challenging limiting beliefs: Recognizing and addressing negative self-talk.
- Creating personalized and impactful affirmations: Tailoring affirmations to specific goals and infusing them with emotion.
- Cultivating a mindset of self-belief: Replacing self-doubt with confidence and embracing challenges.
- Practicing consistent affirmations: Integrating affirmations into daily routines for sustained impact.
- Celebrating progress and appreciating achievements: Recognizing and acknowledging successes.

Emma's journey demonstrates that by harnessing the power of positive thinking, anyone can overcome self-doubt, unlock their full potential, and achieve their dreams.

Chapter 2

THE SCIENCE BEHIND POSITIVE AFFIRMATIONS

Positive affirmations are more than just feel-good phrases; they are potent tools rooted in psychological and neurological science. This chapter delves into the mechanisms that make affirmations effective and how they can transform your mindset and behavior.

THE PSYCHOLOGICAL BASIS

Positive affirmations are grounded in the principles of cognitive-behavioral therapy (CBT). CBT posits that our thoughts, feelings, and behaviors are interconnected. By changing our thoughts, we can influence our emotions and actions. Affirmations work by challenging and replacing negative self-talk with positive statements, fostering a healthier mental state.

THE NEUROLOGICAL PERSPECTIVE

From a neurological standpoint, affirmations can rewire the brain. The brain's neuroplasticity allows it to form new neural pathways in response to repeated thoughts and experiences. You strengthen these new pathways by consistently practicing positive affirmations, making positive thinking more automatic. This process is akin to building muscle through regular exercise.

THE ROLE OF SELF-AFFIRMATION THEORY

The self-affirmation theory suggests that people can maintain self-integrity by affirming their beliefs. Research supports this theory, showing that self-affirmations can reduce stress, improve problem-solving, and enhance overall well-being. Affirming our core values bolsters our resilience against challenges and setbacks.

Scientific Studies and Evidence

Numerous studies have demonstrated the efficacy of positive affirmations. For instance, a study published in the journal *Social Cognitive and Affective Neuroscience* found that self-affirmations activate the brain's reward centers, similar to other pleasurable activities. Another study in *Psychological Science* revealed that affirmations can improve academic performance by reducing stress and anxiety.

Practical Examples of Positive Affirmations

1. **For Self-Confidence**: *"I am confident in my abilities and trust myself to succeed."*

2. **For Stress Reduction:** *"I am calm, centered, and in control of my emotions."*
3. **For Health and Wellness:** *"I am healthy, strong, and energetic."*
4. **For Personal Growth:** *"I am constantly growing and evolving into a better version of myself."*
5. **For Relationships:** *"I am surrounded by love and support from my friends and family."*

Understanding the science behind positive affirmations can help you harness their power more effectively. Remember, consistency is key. The more you practice, the more profound the impact on your mental and emotional well-being.

JOHN'S TRANSFORMATION TO BETTER HEALTH: UNLEASHING THE POWER OF POSITIVE AFFIRMATIONS

John had long struggled with his weight and overall health. He felt trapped in a cycle of unhealthy habits, plagued by self-doubt and a lack of motivation. He tried numerous diets and exercise routines, but nothing seemed to stick. Limiting beliefs like *"I'm not disciplined enough"* and *"I'll never be truly healthy"* constantly sabotaged his efforts.

One day, while reading about the power of the mind, John discovered the potential of positive affirmations. He decided to experiment, crafting affirmations explicitly tailored to his health goals. He started each day with powerful statements: *"I am committed to my health and well-being."* He replaced negative thoughts with positive ones, affirming: *"I make healthy choices that nourish my body and mind."*

At first, it felt awkward and forced, but John persisted. He repeated his affirmations with conviction, gradually infusing them with emotion and visualizing himself achieving his fitness goals. He even wrote his affirmations on sticky notes and placed them around his home and on his fridge, creating constant reminders of his commitment.

He began to challenge his limiting beliefs. Instead of *"I'm not disciplined enough,"* he said, *"I am disciplined and committed to my health journey."* This shift in perspective empowered him to take control of his choices.

John realized that affirmations were just the beginning. He started cultivating a mindful approach to his health. He listened to his body's signals, recognized hunger cues, and practiced intuitive eating. He incorporated enjoyable activities into his routine, discovering a passion for hiking and swimming.

He began to view setbacks as opportunities for learning and growth. Instead of dwelling on missed workouts or occasional indulgences, he used these experiences as reminders to stay focused on his overall progress. He celebrated small victories, such as successfully resisting a tempting treat or completing a challenging workout.

John's dedication and consistent effort began to pay off. He gradually shed weight, his energy levels soared, and he felt a newfound vitality. He noticed improvements in his sleep, mood, and overall well-being. His friends and family were amazed by his transformation, inspired by his dedication and positive attitude.

John attributes his success to the power of affirmations. They gave him the strength and motivation to overcome challenges and stay committed to his health journey. He realized he had unlocked his true potential for a healthier, happier life by changing his mindset.

Today, John continues to use affirmations to maintain his healthy lifestyle. He encourages others to embrace the power of positive thinking, emphasizing the importance of:

- Identifying and challenging limiting beliefs: Recognizing and addressing negative thought patterns.
- Creating personalized and impactful affirmations: Tailoring affirmations to specific goals and infusing them with emotion.
- Cultivating a mindful approach to health: Paying attention to the body and practicing intuitive eating.
- Viewing setbacks as opportunities for growth: Learning from challenges and staying focused on the overall journey.
- Celebrating progress and appreciating achievements: Recognizing and acknowledging successes.

John's story demonstrates that anyone can achieve their health and wellness goals by harnessing the power of positive thinking and taking consistent action.

Chapter 3

Crafting Your Powerful Affirmations

Creating your affirmations is a deeply personal and empowering process. This chapter will guide you through the steps to craft affirmations that resonate with your unique goals and values, ensuring they are both practical and meaningful.

Understanding the Components of Effective Affirmations

1. **Positive Language**: Affirmations should always be framed positively. Instead of focusing on what you want to avoid, emphasize what you want to achieve. For example, say *"I am confident"* rather than *"I am not afraid."*

2. **Present Tense**: Write your affirmations as if they have already been confirmed. This helps to align your subconscious mind with your desired reality. For instance, *"I am successful"* is more powerful than *"I will be successful."*

3. **Specificity**: Be specific about what you want to affirm. Vague affirmations can be less impactful. Instead of saying, *"I am happy,"* you might say, *"I am filled with joy and gratitude daily."*

4. **Emotional Connection**: Your affirmations should evoke positive emotions. The more you feel the affirmation, the more effective it will be. Choose words that resonate deeply with you.

5. **Believability**: Ensure your affirmations are believable to you. If an affirmation feels too far from your current reality, you might struggle to internalize it. Start with something you can genuinely accept and build from there.

STEPS TO CRAFT YOUR AFFIRMATIONS

1. **Identify Your Goals**: Reflect on what you want to achieve in your career, relationships, health, and personal growth.

2. **Write Down Your Goals**: Clearly articulate your goals. This will help you create affirmations that align with your aspirations.

3. **Transform Goals into Affirmations**: Convert each goal into a positive, present-tense statement that is specific, emotionally charged, and believable.

4. **Review and Refine**: Read your affirmations aloud. Adjust any that don't feel right until each one resonates with you.

5. **Practice Regularly**: Consistency is key. Repeat your affirmations daily, ideally in front of a mirror, to reinforce their impact.

Examples of Powerful Affirmations

1. **For Career Success:** *"I am thriving in my career and attracting new opportunities daily."*
2. **For Financial Abundance:** *"I am financially abundant, and money flows to me effortlessly."*
3. **For Self-Love:** *"I am worthy of love and respect, and I honor myself every day."*
4. **For Health and Wellness:** *"I am vibrant, healthy, and energetic."*
5. **For Personal Growth:** *"I am constantly learning and growing, becoming the best version of myself."*

PERSONALIZING YOUR AFFIRMATIONS

Personalize your affirmations with details unique to your life to make them even more powerful. For example, instead of *"I am successful,"* you might say, *"I am a successful personal development coach, inspiring and empowering others daily."*

INCORPORATING AFFIRMATIONS INTO YOUR DAILY ROUTINE

1. **Morning Routine**: Start your day with affirmations to set a positive tone.
2. **Visualization**: Combine affirmations with visualization techniques to enhance their effectiveness.
3. **Journaling**: Write your affirmations in a journal to reinforce them.
4. **Mindfulness Practices**: Integrate affirmations into meditation or mindfulness exercises.

By crafting and regularly practicing your affirmations, you can harness their power to transform your mindset and achieve your goals. Remember, making them personal, positive, and present-focused is key.

Emily's Journey to Financial Abundance: Unleashing the Power of Positive Affirmations

As a single mother of two, Emily juggled multiple jobs, yet financial stress remained a constant companion. Every month, the struggle to make ends meet felt like an uphill battle, leaving her hopeless and trapped. She often grappled with limiting beliefs like *"I'll never be financially secure"* and *"Money is hard to come by."* Deeply ingrained in her subconscious, these beliefs sabotaged her efforts and hindered her progress.

One evening, while browsing online, Emily stumbled upon an article about the power of positive affirmations. Intrigued by the idea that her thoughts could shape her reality, she experimented. She began by identifying and challenging her limiting beliefs. Instead of *"Money is hard to come by,"* she said, *"Abundance flows freely to me."*

She incorporated these affirmations into her daily routine. Every morning, she would stand in front of the mirror, looking herself in the eyes, and declare with conviction: *"I am worthy of financial abundance."* She visualized herself achieving her financial goals, imagining the freedom and security that came with them. She even personalized her affirmations: *"I am a successful entrepreneur, creating valuable products that bring joy to others and prosperity to my family."*

Emily understood that affirmations were just the beginning. She began to cultivate a mindset of abundance, focusing on gratitude for her blessings and appreciating the value of her skills and talents. She started viewing challenges as opportunities for growth and learning.

Inspired by her newfound confidence, Emily decided to turn her passion for crafting into a viable income source. She started small, investing her time and energy into creating high-quality, handmade jewelry and decorative items. She infused each piece with positive energy, believing in their value and the abundance they could attract.

She launched an online store and actively engaged in marketing her products on social media. She networked with other entrepreneurs, learning valuable business skills and seeking support. She embraced continuous learning, researching market trends, and exploring new techniques to improve her craft.

Emily's dedication and positive mindset began to attract customers. She built a loyal following, receiving positive feedback and glowing reviews. This encouraged her to expand her product line and explore new avenues, such as participating in local markets and fairs.

As her business flourished, Emily experienced a surge in confidence and self-belief. She was able to pay off her debts, build a comfortable savings cushion, and provide a better future for her children. She invested in their education, ensuring they had access to quality opportunities.

Looking back, Emily firmly believes that her transformation began with a shift in her mindset. She manifested her financial abundance by challenging her limiting beliefs, cultivating a positive attitude, and taking consistent action. Her journey is a testament to the power of positive thinking, demonstrating that anything is possible with unwavering belief in oneself.

This story highlights the following key elements:

- **Identifying and challenging limiting beliefs**: Recognizing and addressing negative thought patterns.
- **Personalizing and emotionalizing affirmations**: Making affirmations specific and impactful.

- **Cultivating a mindset of abundance**: Focusing on gratitude and appreciating one's value.
- **Taking consistent action**: Transforming thoughts into tangible results through dedicated effort.
- **Embracing continuous learning and growth**: Adapting and evolving to overcome challenges.
- **Celebrating success and appreciating progress**: Recognizing and acknowledging achievements.

Emily's story inspires, demonstrating that anyone can overcome financial challenges and create a life of abundance and prosperity with a positive mindset and consistent effort.

Chapter 4

Daily Practices to Integrate Affirmations into Your Life

Integrating positive affirmations into your daily routine can significantly enhance their effectiveness. This chapter explores various practices to seamlessly incorporate affirmations into your life, ensuring they become a natural and influential part of your daily habits.

Morning Rituals

1. **Morning Affirmation Routine**: Start your day with a set of affirmations. Stand before a mirror, look yourself in the eyes, and recite your affirmations with conviction. This practice sets a positive tone for the day ahead.
   Example: *"I am confident, capable, and ready to tackle any challenges today."*

2. **Affirmation Journaling**: Dedicate a few minutes each morning to writing down your affirmations. This will reinforce your intentions and help you start the day with a focused mindset. **For example**, *"I am grateful for the abundance in my life and welcome more each day."*

THROUGHOUT THE DAY

1. **Affirmation Reminders**: Set reminders on your phone or place sticky notes in visible areas (like your workspace or car) to prompt you to repeat your affirmations throughout the day. **Example**: *"I am productive and efficient in all my tasks."*

2. **Mindful Breathing with Affirmations**: Combine affirmations with deep breathing exercises. As you inhale, silently repeat an affirmation. As you

exhale, release any tension or negativity. **For example,** Inhale, *"I am calm and centered."* Exhale, *"I release stress and tension."*

3. **Affirmation Breaks**: Take short breaks during your day to recite your affirmations. This can be especially helpful during stressful moments or before essential tasks. **Example:** *"I am prepared and confident for this meeting."*

EVENING PRACTICES

1. **Evening Reflection**: Before bed, reflect on your day and recite affirmations reinforcing your achievements and setting positive intentions for tomorrow. **For example,** *"I am proud of my accomplishments today and look forward to new opportunities tomorrow."*

2. **Gratitude and Affirmation Journal:** Combine gratitude journaling with affirmations. Write down things you are grateful for and follow them with affirmations that align with your gratitude. **For example,** *"I am grateful for my supportive friends and affirm that I am surrounded by love and positivity."*

INTEGRATING AFFIRMATIONS INTO ACTIVITIES

1. **Exercise and Affirmations:** Incorporate affirmations into your workout routine. Repeat affirmations that motivate and empower you as you exercise. **Example:** *"I am strong, healthy, and energetic."*

2. **Affirmations During Chores:** Use routine tasks like cooking or cleaning as opportunities to recite affirmations. This turns mundane activities into moments of positive reinforcement.

Example: *"I am organized and efficient in all I do."*

VISUALIZATION TECHNIQUES

1. **Visualization with Affirmations**: Pair your affirmations with visualization. Close your eyes and vividly imagine the affirmation as your reality. This strengthens the connection between your mind and your goals. **Example:** *"I am living my dream life, filled with joy and success."*

2. **Vision Board**: Create a vision board with images and words representing your affirmations. Place it where you can see it daily to keep your goals and affirmations in focus. Include pictures of success, health, and happiness that align with your affirmations.

AFFIRMATIONS IN MEDITATION

1. **Affirmation Meditation**: Dedicate part of your meditation practice to repeating affirmations. This can deepen your focus and reinforce positive beliefs. **Example**: *"I am at peace with myself and the world around me."*

2. **Guided Affirmation Meditations**: Use guided meditations that incorporate affirmations. These can be found in apps or online, providing a structured way to integrate affirmations into your meditation practice. **For example,** Follow a guided meditation that focuses on self-love and acceptance.

By incorporating these daily practices, you can make affirmations a natural and influential part of your life. Consistency and repetition are crucial to harnessing their full potential, helping you to cultivate a positive mindset and achieve your goals.

AFFIRMING LOVE: MARK'S JOURNEY TO CONNECTION

Mark had always felt like an outsider, navigating social gatherings with a hidden void. Despite having many acquaintances, he yearned for deep, meaningful connections. He often felt disconnected, believing he wasn't worthy of true love and understanding. This belief manifested in his interactions, leaving him feeling lonely and isolated.

Determined to break this pattern, Mark embarked on a journey of self-discovery. He began by delving into his core needs: love, connection, and belonging. He recognized that his limiting beliefs - *"I'm not good enough"* and *"People don't truly understand me"* - hindered his ability to form authentic bonds.

To counter these beliefs, Mark embraced the power of affirmations. Every morning, he stood before the mirror, looked into his eyes, and declared, *"I am worthy of deep and fulfilling love."* He replaced broad statements with personalized affirmations, such as, *"I am open to experiencing the joy of deep, authentic love with someone who shares my values."* He infused these affirmations with emotion, visualizing himself surrounded by loving and supportive friends.

He plastered his affirmations on sticky notes around his home, constantly reminding himself of his commitment to change. He even started framing his affirmations in the present tense, declaring, *"Loving and supportive friends surround me."* This shift in perspective helped him believe in the possibility of change.

But Mark knew that affirmations alone were not enough. He began practicing mindful presence in his interactions, actively listening, and showing genuine interest in others. He started sharing his true self with vulnerability, acknowledging his fears and desires. He joined a local book club, finding a community that shared his passion for literature.

Within this supportive environment, Mark began to blossom. He engaged in meaningful discussions, sharing his thoughts and feelings openly. He met Sarah, a kind-hearted individual who shared his love for travel and storytelling. They connected deeply, sharing their dreams and fears with authenticity.

Mark cultivated a circle of friends who uplifted and inspired him, celebrating his victories and offering support during challenging times. He expressed kindness and generosity, engaging in small acts of service that strengthened his bonds with others.

Occasionally, Mark would reflect on his journey, acknowledging and appreciating every step forward. He celebrated small victories, like a deeper conversation or a newfound connection, and used these successes to motivate and inspire himself further.

Mark's transformation wasn't overnight. It was a gradual process of self-discovery, consistent effort, and a genuine desire for growth. He learned that affirmations and mindful action could unlock the potential for deep and fulfilling relationships. He shared his journey with others, encouraging them to embrace the power of their thoughts and words and believe in their ability to create the life they desire.

Mark's story is a testament to the transformative power of self-belief and the importance of cultivating a positive mindset. By addressing his core needs, challenging his limiting beliefs, and practicing mindful presence, he was able to break free from isolation and build a life filled with love and connection.

This story emphasizes the importance of:
- Identifying and addressing core needs.
- Challenging limiting beliefs.
- Personalizing and emotionalizing affirmations.
- Practicing mindful presence and vulnerability.
- Cultivating a supportive community.
- Celebrating progress and embracing the journey.

By incorporating these principles into their lives, readers can cultivate more fulfilling and meaningful relationships, just as Mark did.

Chapter 5

Overcoming Negative Self-Talk

Negative self-talk can be a significant barrier to personal growth and happiness. This chapter explores strategies for identifying, challenging, and replacing negative self-talk with empowering affirmations, helping you cultivate a more positive and supportive inner dialogue.

Understanding Negative Self-Talk

Negative self-talk refers to our critical and often irrational thoughts about ourselves. These thoughts can undermine our confidence, increase stress, and hinder our ability to achieve our goals. Typical forms of negative self-talk include:

1. **Catastrophizing**: Expecting the worst-case scenario.
2. **Personalizing**: Blaming yourself for things outside your control.
3. **Filtering**: Focusing only on the negative aspects of a situation.
4. **Polarizing**: Seeing things in black-and-white terms without recognizing the gray areas.

IDENTIFYING NEGATIVE SELF-TALK

The first step in overcoming negative self-talk is to become aware of it. Pay attention to your inner dialogue and notice when you are being self-critical. Keeping a journal can help you track these thoughts and identify patterns.

Challenging Negative Self-Talk

Once you have identified negative self-talk, the next step is to challenge it. Ask yourself the following questions:

1. Is this thought based on facts or assumptions?
2. Would I say this to a friend?
3. What evidence do I have that contradicts this thought?
4. Is there a more positive or realistic way to view this situation?

Replacing Negative Self-Talk with Positive Affirmations

After challenging negative thoughts, replace them with positive affirmations. Here are some strategies to help you craft effective affirmations:

1. **Acknowledge the Negative Thought:** Recognize negative thoughts without judgment. This helps neutralize their power. **Example:** Negative Thought: *"I always mess things up."* **Acknowledgment:** *"I notice that I'm being hard on myself."*

2. **Create a Positive Counterstatement:** Transform the negative thought into a positive affirmation that reflects a more balanced and supportive perspective. **Example:** Positive Affirmation: *"I can learn from my mistakes and improve."*

3. **Use Evidence-Based Affirmations:** To make your affirmations more believable, base them on facts and past successes. For e**xample**, *"I have completed challenging tasks before and can do it again."*

4. **Practice Self-Compassion:** Incorporate affirmations that promote self-compassion and kindness. **Example:** *"I am doing my best, which is enough."*

EXAMPLES OF TRANSFORMING NEGATIVE SELF-TALK

1. **Negative Self-Talk:** *"I am not good enough."* **Positive Affirmation:** *"I am worthy and capable of achieving my goals."*

2. **Negative Self-Talk:** *"I always fail."* **Positive Affirmation:** *"I learn and grow from every experience."*

3. **Negative Self-Talk:** *"No one likes me."* **Positive Affirmation:** *"I am surrounded by people who appreciate and support me."*

4. **Negative Self-Talk**: *"I can't handle this."* **Positive Affirmation**: *"I am strong and resilient and can overcome any challenge."*

DAILY PRACTICES TO OVERCOME NEGATIVE SELF-TALK

1. **Mindfulness Meditation**: Practice mindfulness to become more aware of your thoughts and to create space between yourself and your negative self-talk. **For example**, Spend a few minutes each day observing your thoughts without judgment.

2. **Affirmation Journaling**: Write down your negative thoughts and their corresponding positive affirmations. This helps to reinforce the new, positive beliefs.

    Example: *"Today, I noticed I was thinking 'I can't do this,' and I replaced it with 'I am capable and resourceful.'"*

3. **Visualization**: Visualize yourself succeeding and embodying the qualities you affirm. This strengthens the connection between your affirmations and your reality. **Example**: Imagine yourself confidently handling a challenging situation.

4. **Supportive Environment**: Surround yourself with positive influences, such as supportive friends, uplifting books, and motivational content. **Example**: Join a community or group that encourages positive thinking and personal growth.

By consistently practicing these strategies, you can transform negative self-talk into a powerful tool for personal development. Remember, overcoming negative self-talk is a journey; every step brings you closer to a more positive and empowered mindset.

Liam: The Athlete's Triumph

Liam, a promising young athlete, felt the weight of expectation pressing down on him. He possessed immense talent, yet the fear of failure often crippled him during competitions.

Limiting beliefs, such as *"I'm not good enough under pressure"* and *"I'm afraid to disappoint my team,"* constantly plagued his mind. This anxiety manifested in his performance, leading to subpar results despite his best efforts.

His coach, noticing his struggle, suggested he explore the power of positive affirmations. Initially skeptical, Liam decided to try it. He started by identifying and challenging his limiting beliefs. Instead of saying, *"I'm afraid to fail,"* he began affirming, *"I embrace challenges and learn from every experience."*

He incorporated these affirmations into his daily routine. Every morning, he visualized himself performing at his peak, feeling confident and in control. He repeated affirmations like, *"I am a strong and resilient athlete,"* and *"I focus on my strengths and perform with unwavering confidence."*

Liam began to notice a subtle shift in his mindset. He felt more relaxed and focused during training sessions. He started to view competitions as opportunities for growth and self-improvement rather than sources of anxiety. He embraced challenges, learning from his mistakes and using them as motivation to improve.

During his next competition, Liam experienced calm and confidence that he had never experienced before. He focused on his strengths, executed his skills precisely, and achieved a personal best. This victory boosted his confidence, and he continued to use affirmations to enhance his performance and achieve his athletic goals.

Key Takeaways:
- Overcoming performance anxiety: Challenging limiting beliefs and replacing them with empowering affirmations.
- Cultivating a growth mindset: Viewing challenges as opportunities for learning and improvement.
- Enhancing focus and performance: Using affirmations to improve mental clarity and reduce distractions.

Chapter 6

AFFIRMATIONS FOR PERSONAL GROWTH AND SELF-LOVE

Personal growth and self-love are foundational to living a fulfilling and empowered life. This chapter explores how affirmations can nurture these aspects, helping you to build a strong sense of self-worth and continuously evolve into your best self.

THE IMPORTANCE OF PERSONAL GROWTH AND SELF-LOVE

Personal growth involves a commitment to self-improvement, learning, and development. It encompasses various areas of life, including emotional, intellectual, and spiritual growth. Self-love, on the other hand, is about accepting and valuing yourself unconditionally.

It means treating yourself with kindness, respect, and compassion.

Affirmations are crucial in fostering personal growth and self-love. They help reframe negative beliefs, reinforce positive self-perceptions, and motivate people to pursue their goals confidently and resiliently.

CRAFTING AFFIRMATIONS FOR PERSONAL GROWTH

1. **Identify Areas for Growth**: Reflect on the areas where you want to grow. This could include skills, habits, or personal qualities.

2. **Set Clear Intentions**: Define your goals and aspirations in these areas.

3. **Create Positive Statements**: Transform your intentions into positive, present-tense affirmations that resonate with you.

EXAMPLES OF AFFIRMATIONS FOR PERSONAL GROWTH

1. **For Learning and Development**: *"I am constantly learning and expanding my knowledge."*
2. **For Resilience**: *"I embrace challenges as opportunities for growth and learning."*
3. **For Creativity**: *"I am a creative thinker, and my ideas are valuable and innovative."*
4. **For Goal Achievement**: *"I am focused and determined to achieve my goals."*
5. **For Adaptability**: *"I am flexible and open to new experiences and opportunities."*

CRAFTING AFFIRMATIONS FOR SELF-LOVE

1. **Acknowledge Your Worth**: Recognize your inherent value and worthiness. Affirmations reflect your self-acceptance and appreciation.

2. **Focus on Self-Compassion**: Create affirmations that encourage kindness and compassion towards yourself, especially during difficult times.

3. **Celebrate Your Qualities**: In affirmations, highlight your strengths, talents, and positive attributes.

EXAMPLES OF AFFIRMATIONS FOR SELF-LOVE

1. **For Self-Acceptance**: *"I love and accept myself exactly as I am."*
2. **For Self-Compassion**: *"I am gentle and compassionate with myself, especially when I make mistakes."*

3. **For Self-Respect**: *"I honor my needs and set healthy boundaries."*
4. **For Self-Worth**: *"I am worthy of love, respect, and happiness."*
5. **For Self-Care**: *"I prioritize my well-being and take care of myself every day."*

Integrating Affirmations into Your Daily Life

1. **Morning Routine**: Start your day with affirmations that set a positive tone for personal growth and self-love. **Example**: *"I am excited to learn and grow today."*

2. **Affirmation Journal**: Keep a journal where you write down your affirmations daily. Reflect on your progress and celebrate your achievements. **Example**: *"Today, I acknowledged my progress in becoming more resilient."*

3. **Mirror Work**: Stand in front of a mirror and recite your affirmations. Look yourself in the eyes and speak with conviction. **Example**: *"I am proud of who I am and who I am becoming."*

4. **Visualization**: Pair your affirmations with visualization techniques. Imagine yourself embodying the qualities you affirm and achieving the goals you establish. **For example**, Visualize yourself confidently navigating a challenging situation.

5. **Mindfulness Practices**: Incorporate affirmations into your meditation or mindfulness routines. This helps reinforce positive beliefs and cultivate a sense of inner peace. **For example**, during meditation, repeat the affirmation, *"I am at peace with myself and my journey."*

By consistently practicing these affirmations, you can nurture a deep sense of self-love and grow into your best self. Remember, the journey of personal growth and self-love is ongoing, and affirmations are powerful tools for support.

Sarah: The Student's Academic Breakthrough

Sarah was a bright student with immense academic potential, yet exam anxiety often held her back. The thought of tests would trigger a wave of anxiety, leading to mental blocks and poor performance. Limiting beliefs like *"I'm not intelligent enough"* and *"I'm afraid of making mistakes"* constantly haunted her.

Her tutor, noticing her struggle, suggested she explore the power of positive affirmations. Sarah was initially hesitant, but she decided to give it a try. She started by identifying and challenging her limiting beliefs. Instead of *"I'm afraid of making mistakes,"* she said, *"I learn from my mistakes and use them as opportunities for growth."*

She incorporated these affirmations into her daily routine. Before each exam, she would repeat affirmations like, *"I am a capable and intelligent student,"* and *"I approach exams confidently and easily."* She visualizes herself calmly and confidently, answers questions, and achieves her academic goals.

Sarah began to notice a significant shift in her mindset. She felt more relaxed and focused during exams, allowing her to access her full potential. She started to view exams as opportunities to demonstrate her knowledge and learning rather than as sources of stress.

With consistent practice, Sarah's academic performance improved dramatically. She felt more confident in her abilities, and her grades reflected this newfound self-belief. She realized that changing her mindset had unlocked her true academic potential.

Key Takeaways:

- Overcoming test anxiety: Replacing fear and self-doubt with confidence and calmness.
- Improving academic performance: Enhancing focus, concentration, and cognitive function.
- Cultivating a growth mindset: Viewing challenges as opportunities for learning and improvement.

Chapter 7

USING AFFIRMATIONS TO ACHIEVE CAREER SUCCESS

This chapter will explore how positive affirmations can be a powerful tool for propelling your career forward. Whether aiming for a promotion, seeking a new job, or striving to excel in your current role, affirmations can help you align your mindset with your career goals. By consistently practicing affirmations, you can overcome self-doubt, build confidence, and attract opportunities that align with your professional aspirations.

THE POWER OF POSITIVE AFFIRMATIONS IN YOUR CAREER

Positive affirmations are statements that reinforce your belief in your abilities and potential. When used effectively, they can help you:

- **Boost Confidence**: Affirmations can help you believe in your skills and capabilities, increasing your confidence in your professional interactions.
- **Enhance Focus**: Repeating affirmations can help you keep your career goals at the forefront of your mind, helping you stay focused and motivated.
- **Reduce Stress**: Positive affirmations can help you manage work-related stress by promoting a positive mindset and reducing negative self-talk.
- **Attract Opportunities**: Affirmations can help you cultivate a mindset that attracts new opportunities and opens doors to career advancement.

CRAFTING EFFECTIVE CAREER AFFIRMATIONS

To create powerful career affirmations, follow these guidelines:

1. **Be Specific**: Tailor your affirmations to your specific career goals and aspirations.
2. **Use Present Tense**: Phrase your affirmations as if they are already confirmed, which helps reinforce the belief that you are already on your way to achieving your goals.
3. **Keep It Positive**: Focus on what you want to achieve rather than what you want to avoid.
4. **Make It Personal**: Use "I" statements to make your affirmations personal and relevant to you.

EXAMPLES OF CAREER SUCCESS AFFIRMATIONS

Here are some examples of affirmations that can help you achieve career success:

1. **Confidence and Self-Belief**
   - *"I am confident in my abilities and skills."*
   - *"I am a valuable asset to my team and organization."*
   - *"I believe in my potential to achieve great things in my career."*

2. **Goal Achievement**
   - *"I am focused and determined to achieve my career goals."*
   - *"I am open to new opportunities that align with my career aspirations."*
   - *"I am constantly growing and improving in my professional life."*

3. Overcoming Challenges

- *"I embrace challenges as opportunities for growth and learning."*
- *"I am resilient and can handle any obstacles that come my way."*
- *"I trust in my ability to solve any problem."*

4. Work-Life Balance

- *"I maintain a healthy balance between my work and personal life."*
- *"I prioritize my well-being and take time to recharge."*
- *"I am productive and efficient in my work, allowing me to enjoy my time."*

5. Attracting Success

- *"I attract success and abundance in my career."*
- *"Supportive and inspiring colleagues surround me."*
- *"I am open to receiving recognition and rewards for my hard work."*

Incorporating Affirmations into Your Daily Routine

To maximize the impact of your affirmations, incorporate them into your daily routine. Here are some tips:

- **Morning Routine**: Start your day with affirmations to set a positive tone for the day ahead.
- **Visualization**: Combine affirmations with visualization techniques to create a vivid mental image of your success.
- **Journaling**: Write down your affirmations to reinforce your commitment to your goals.
- **Reminders**: Keep affirmation reminders in visible locations, such as your workspace or phone, so that you can remember them throughout the day.

By consistently practicing these affirmations, you can cultivate a positive mindset that supports your career growth and success. Remember, the key to effective affirmations is repetition and belief. Trust in the power of your words and watch as they transform your professional life.

MARK: THE ARTIST'S CREATIVE BREAKTHROUGH

Mark, a talented artist, felt stifled by creative blocks. He often stared at a blank canvas, plagued by self-doubt and the fear of creating something mediocre. Limiting beliefs like *"I'm not original enough"* and *"My art is not good enough"* constantly crept into his mind, hindering his creative flow.

He decided to explore the power of affirmations to overcome his creative block. He started by identifying and challenging his limiting beliefs. Instead of *"My art is not good enough,"* he began affirming, *"My art is unique and meaningful, and I express myself authentically."*

He incorporated these affirmations into his daily routine. Every morning, he visualized himself immersed in the creative process, ideas flowing freely and effortlessly. He repeated affirmations like, *"I am a creative and imaginative artist,"* and *"I trust my intuition and allow my creativity to flow freely."*

Mark began to notice a shift in his creative process. He felt more open to new ideas and less afraid to experiment. He started to view creative blocks as opportunities for exploration and growth rather than obstacles to overcome.

He began producing more original and impactful work. He felt renewed passion and joy in his art and expressed himself with greater authenticity and confidence. Mark realized he had unlocked his creative potential by cultivating a positive and supportive inner dialogue.

Key Takeaways:

- Overcoming creative blocks: Fostering a more positive and supportive inner dialogue.
- Enhancing creativity and inspiration: Unleashing the flow of ideas and encouraging artistic expression.
- Building confidence in artistic abilities: Overcoming self-doubt and embracing one's unique creative voice.

Chapter 8

Health and Wellness: Affirmations for a Balanced Life

This chapter will explore the importance of health and wellness and how positive affirmations can help achieve a balanced life. Health and wellness encompass physical well-being and mental and emotional health. By integrating affirmations into your daily routine, you can foster a holistic approach to wellness that nurtures your body, mind, and spirit.

The Role of Affirmations in Health and Wellness

Positive affirmations can significantly impact your health and wellness by:

- **Promoting a Positive Mindset:** Affirmations help shift your focus from negative thoughts to positive ones,

which can improve your overall mental health.
- **Encouraging Healthy Habits**: Repeating affirmations can reinforce your commitment to healthy behaviors, such as regular exercise and balanced nutrition.
- **Reducing Stress**: Affirmations can help you manage stress by promoting relaxation and a sense of calm.
- **Enhancing Self-Love**: Affirmations encourage self-acceptance and self-compassion, essential for emotional well-being.

CRAFTING EFFECTIVE HEALTH AND WELLNESS AFFIRMATIONS

To create robust health and wellness affirmations, consider the following tips:

1. **Be Specific**: Tailor your affirmations to your specific health and wellness goals.

2. **Use Present Tense**: Phrase your affirmations as if they are already true to reinforce the belief that you are already on your way to achieving your goals.
3. **Keep It Positive**: Focus on what you want to achieve rather than what you want to avoid.
4. **Make It Personal**: Use "I" statements to make your affirmations personal and relevant to you.

Examples of Health and Wellness Affirmations

Here are some examples of affirmations that can help you achieve a balanced and healthy life:

1. **Physical Health**
   - *"I am strong, healthy, and full of energy."*

- "I nourish my body with healthy foods and regular exercise."
- "I listen to my body's needs and care for them with love and respect."

2. **Mental Health**
   - "I am in control of my thoughts and emotions."
   - "I choose to focus on the positive aspects of my life."
   - "I am resilient and can handle any challenges that come my way."

3. **Emotional Well-Being**
   - "I am worthy of love and happiness."
   - "I forgive myself and others, releasing any negative emotions."
   - "I am at peace with myself and my surroundings."

4. **Stress Management**
   - "I remain calm and centered in stressful situations."
   - "I relax and recharge my mind and body."

- *"I control my stress levels and easily handle them."*

5. Holistic Wellness

- *"I am balanced in mind, body, and spirit."*
- *"I prioritize my well-being and make time for self-care."*
- *"I am grateful for my health and the ability to improve it daily."*

INCORPORATING AFFIRMATIONS INTO YOUR DAILY ROUTINE

To maximize the impact of your affirmations, incorporate them into your daily routine. Here are some tips:

- **Morning Routine:** Start your day with affirmations to set a positive tone for the day ahead.

- **Visualization**: Combine affirmations with visualization techniques to create a vivid mental image of your health and wellness goals.
- **Journaling**: Write down your affirmations to reinforce your commitment to your goals.

Place affirmation reminders in visible locations, such as your bathroom mirror or phone, to keep them top of mind throughout the day.

By consistently practicing these affirmations, you can cultivate a positive mindset that supports your overall health and wellness. Remember, the key to effective affirmations is repetition and belief. Trust in the power of your words and watch as they transform your life.

Sandra: The Entrepreneur's Success

Sandra, a budding entrepreneur, was brimming with passion and innovative ideas, yet fear and self-doubt often threatened to derail her. Launching a new business was daunting – fearing failure, financial insecurity, and the constant pressure to succeed.

Limiting beliefs, such as *"I'm not a good enough businesswoman"* and *"My business will fail,"* constantly crept into her mind.

Determined to overcome these obstacles, Sandra explored the power of affirmations. She started by identifying and challenging her limiting beliefs. Instead of *"My business will fail,"* she said, *"My business is a success, and I am achieving my entrepreneurial goals."*

She incorporated these affirmations into her daily routine. Every morning, she would visualize her business thriving, attracting customers, and achieving its full potential.

She repeated affirmations like, *"I am a successful entrepreneur, and my business is a thriving and growing entity."* She even wrote her affirmations on sticky notes and placed them around her workspace, constantly reminding herself of her goals.

Sandra began to notice a shift in her mindset. She felt more confident in her abilities and approached challenges with a proactive, solution-oriented approach. She started to view setbacks as learning opportunities, using them to refine her business strategy and improve her offerings.

Her positive mindset attracted opportunities. She networked with other entrepreneurs, built strong client relationships, and consistently delivered high-quality products and services. Her business began to grow steadily, exceeding her initial expectations.

Sandra realized that her affirmations had been crucial to her success. They had given her the strength and resilience to overcome challenges, stay focused on her goals, and achieve her entrepreneurial dreams.

Key Takeaways:
- Overcoming fear of failure and self-doubt: Building confidence and resilience in facing challenges.
- Attracting opportunities: Cultivating a positive and magnetic energy that attracts success.
- Building a strong and successful business: Fostering a growth mindset and embracing challenges as opportunities.

This story provides valuable insights into how affirmations can empower individuals to achieve their goals and live fulfilling lives!

Chapter 9

FINANCIAL ABUNDANCE: MANIFESTING WEALTH THROUGH POSITIVE THOUGHTS

This chapter will explore how positive affirmations can help you manifest financial abundance and create a prosperous life. Financial abundance is about having money and cultivating a mindset that attracts wealth and opportunities. By using affirmations, you can shift your thoughts and beliefs towards economic success, paving the way for a more abundant and fulfilling life.

THE POWER OF POSITIVE AFFIRMATIONS IN FINANCIAL ABUNDANCE

Positive affirmations can significantly impact your financial well-being by:

- **Changing Your Money Mindset:** Affirmations help you develop a positive relationship with money, replacing limiting beliefs with empowering ones.
- **Attracting Opportunities:** By focusing on abundance, you open yourself up to new opportunities for wealth and success.
- **Building Confidence:** Affirmations can boost your confidence in managing and growing your finances.
- **Reducing Financial Stress:** Positive affirmations can help alleviate money-related anxiety and stress, promoting financial security.

CRAFTING EFFECTIVE FINANCIAL ABUNDANCE AFFIRMATIONS

To create powerful financial abundance affirmations, consider the following tips:

1. **Be Specific**: Customize your affirmations to your specific financial goals and aspirations.
2. **Use Present Tense**: Phrase your affirmations as if they are already true to reinforce the belief that you are already on your way to achieving your goals.
3. **Keep It Positive**: Focus on what you want to achieve rather than what you want to avoid.
4. **Make It Personal**: Use "I" statements to make your affirmations personal and relevant to you.

EXAMPLES OF FINANCIAL ABUNDANCE AFFIRMATIONS

Here are some examples of affirmations that can help you manifest financial abundance:

1. **Wealth and Prosperity**
    - *"I am a magnet for wealth and prosperity."*
    - *"Money flows to me easily and effortlessly."*
    - *"I am open to receiving unlimited abundance."*

2. **Financial Confidence**
    - *"I am confident in my ability to manage and grow my finances."*
    - *"I make wise financial decisions that lead to success."*
    - *"I trust in my ability to create financial stability."*

3. **Attracting Opportunities**
    - *"I attract lucrative opportunities that align with my financial goals."*
    - *"I am open to new and exciting sources of income."*
    - *"I am surrounded by opportunities to create wealth."*

4. **Financial Security**
    - *"I am financially secure and stable."*
    - *"I have more than enough money to meet my needs and desires."*
    - *"I am grateful for the financial abundance in my life."*

5. **Abundance Mindset**
    - *"I believe in my ability to create and sustain financial abundance."*
    - *"I am worthy of financial success and prosperity."*
    - *"I am aligned with the energy of abundance."*

INCORPORATING AFFIRMATIONS INTO YOUR DAILY ROUTINE

To maximize the impact of your affirmations, incorporate them into your daily routine. Here are some tips:

- **Morning Routine**: Start your day with affirmations to set a positive tone for the day ahead.
- **Visualization**: Combine affirmations with visualization techniques to create a vivid mental image of your financial goals.
- **Journaling**: Write down your affirmations to reinforce your commitment to your goals.
- **Reminders**: Place affirmation reminders in visible locations, such as your wallet or phone, to keep them at the top of your mind throughout the day.

By consistently practicing these affirmations, you can cultivate a positive mindset that supports your financial growth and success. Remember, the key to effective affirmations is repetition and belief. Trust in the power of your words and watch as they transform your financial life.

Larry: The Overcomer of Social Anxiety

Larry, a naturally introverted individual, lived with a constant shadow of social anxiety. He dreaded social gatherings, fearing judgment and rejection at every turn. This fear limited his interactions, hindering his ability to form meaningful connections and experience the joy of genuine human interaction. Limiting beliefs like *"I'm not interesting enough"* and "People won't like me" constantly fueled his anxiety.

Desperate to break free from this cycle, Larry explored the power of affirmations. He started by identifying and challenging his limiting beliefs. Instead of *"People won't like me,"* he said, *"I am worthy of love and acceptance, and I attract positive and supportive relationships."*

He incorporated these affirmations into his daily routine. Every morning, he visualized himself confidently engaging in social situations and feeling relaxed and comfortable. He would repeat affirmations like, *"I am confident and comfortable in social situations,"* and *"I express myself authentically and connect with others on a deeper level."*

Larry began to notice subtle shifts in his behavior. He started stepping outside his comfort zone, attending small gatherings, and conversing briefly. He also practiced active listening, focused on others, and showed genuine interest in their lives.

He used affirmations to counter his anxiety during social situations. Whenever fear or self-doubt arose, he would silently repeat his affirmations, reminding himself of his worth and ability to connect with others.

Gradually, Larry's social anxiety began to diminish. He started to enjoy social interactions, forming meaningful friendships, and experiencing the joy of genuine human connection. He realized that by changing his mindset and challenging his limiting beliefs, he had overcome his social anxiety and opened himself up to a world of possibilities.

Key Takeaways:
- Overcoming social anxiety: Building self-confidence and reducing fear of judgment.
- Improving social skills: Enhancing communication, active listening, and social interaction.
- Building meaningful relationships: Attracting positive and supportive connections.

Chapter 10

BUILDING MEANINGFUL RELATIONSHIPS WITH AFFIRMATIONS

In this chapter, we will explore how positive affirmations can enhance your relationships, whether they are with family, friends, colleagues, or romantic partners. Building meaningful relationships requires effort, understanding, and a positive mindset. Affirmations can help you cultivate the qualities to foster deep and lasting connections with others.

THE ROLE OF AFFIRMATIONS IN BUILDING RELATIONSHIPS

Positive affirmations can significantly impact your relationships by:

- **Enhancing Communication**: Affirmations can help you become a better

communicator, expressing your thoughts and feelings clearly and effectively.
- **Fostering Empathy**: By focusing on positive qualities, affirmations can help you develop empathy and understanding towards others.
- **Building Trust**: Affirmations can reinforce your commitment to honesty and integrity, which are essential for building trust.
- **Promoting Positivity**: Affirmations can help you maintain a positive attitude, improving your interactions with others.

CRAFTING EFFECTIVE RELATIONSHIP AFFIRMATIONS

To create powerful relationship affirmations, consider the following tips:

1. **Be Specific**: Tailor your affirmations to the qualities you want to cultivate in your relationships.

2. **Use Present Tense**: Phrase your affirmations as if they are already true to reinforce the belief that you already embody these qualities.
3. **Keep It Positive**: Focus on what you want to achieve rather than what you want to avoid.
4. **Make It Personal**: Use "I" statements to make your affirmations personal and relevant to you.

Examples of Relationship Affirmations

Here are some examples of affirmations that can help you build meaningful relationships:

1. **Communication**
    - *"I communicate my thoughts and feelings with clarity and confidence."*
    - *"I listen actively, and I am empathetic to others."*

- *"I express myself honestly and respectfully."*

2. Empathy and Understanding

- *"I am compassionate and understanding towards others."*
- *"I seek to understand before being understood."*
- *"I am patient and considerate in my interactions."*

3. Trust and Integrity

- *"I am trustworthy and reliable in my relationships."*
- *"I honor my commitments and promises."*
- *"I build trust through honesty and integrity."*

4. Positivity and Support

- *"I bring positivity and joy to my relationships."*
- *"I support and uplift those around me."*
- *"I am a source of encouragement and inspiration."*

5. **Love and Connection**
   - *"I am open to giving and receiving love."*
   - *"I nurture deep and meaningful connections with others."*
   - *"I am grateful for the loving relationships in my life."*

INCORPORATING AFFIRMATIONS INTO YOUR DAILY ROUTINE

To maximize the impact of your affirmations, incorporate them into your daily routine. Here are some tips:

- **Morning Routine:** Start your day with affirmations to set a positive tone for your interactions.
- **Visualization:** Combine affirmations with visualization techniques to create a vivid mental image of your ideal relationships.

- **Journaling**: Write down your affirmations in a journal to reinforce your commitment to building meaningful relationships.
- **Reminders**: Keep affirmation reminders in visible locations, such as your workspace or phone, so that you can remember them throughout the day.

By consistently practicing these affirmations, you can cultivate a positive mindset that supports the development of meaningful and fulfilling relationships. Remember, the key to effective affirmations is repetition and belief. Trust in the power of your words and watch as they transform your connections with others.

MAYA: THE SEEKER OF INNER PEACE

Maya lived in a constant state of stress and anxiety, the demands of her fast-paced life leaving her feeling overwhelmed and depleted. She craved inner peace and a sense of balance but felt constantly bombarded by external pressures. Limiting beliefs like *"I'm not good at managing stress"* and *"I'm always feeling overwhelmed"* contributed to her anxiety.

Determined to find inner peace, Maya explored the power of affirmations. She started by identifying and challenging her limiting beliefs. Instead of *"I'm not good at managing stress,"* she began affirming, *"I am capable of managing stress effectively and maintaining inner peace."*

She incorporated these affirmations into her daily routine. She practiced mindfulness techniques, such as deep breathing and meditation, while repeating affirmations like, *"I am calm, centered, and at peace,"*

99

and *"I release stress and embrace tranquility."*

Maya began to notice a shift in her perception of stress. She started viewing challenges as opportunities for growth and learned to respond to stressful situations with more excellent composure. She developed healthy coping mechanisms like spending time in nature, engaging in creative activities, and prioritizing self-care.

As her inner peace deepened, Maya felt more grounded and centered in her daily life. She experienced renewed joy and fulfillment, appreciating simple pleasures and cultivating greater well-being.

Key Takeaways:
- Reducing stress and anxiety: Cultivating inner peace and a sense of calm.
- Improving emotional well-being: Developing healthy coping mechanisms and enhancing emotional resilience.

- Finding more excellent balance and fulfillment: Appreciating simple pleasures and prioritizing self-care.

I hope these featured stories provide further insights into the transformative power of personalized positive affirmations!

How to Create Your Own Success Story

These real-life examples throughout this book show that affirmations can powerfully impact various aspects of life. To create your own success story, follow these steps:

1. **Identify Your Goals**: Determine the specific areas of your life where you want to see improvement.
2. **Craft Personalized Affirmations**: Create specific, positive, relevant affirmations for your goals.
3. **Practice Consistently**: Repeat your affirmations daily, incorporating them into your routine.
4. **Believe in the Process**: Trust in the power of your words and maintain a positive mindset.
5. **Take Action**: Combine affirmations with actionable steps towards your goals.

Following these steps and staying committed to affirmations can create your success story and transform your life meaningfully.

Chapter 11

Epilogue: The Tapestry of Transformation

We've journeyed together through stories of resilience, courage, and the quiet power of self-belief. Each narrative, a thread in the rich tapestry of human experience, has illuminated the potential within each of us. Like the characters you've encountered, you, too, possess the ability to rewrite your story, to move from a place of doubt to a realm of boundless possibility.

Remember Sarah, who found her voice amidst the noise of self-criticism? Her journey reminds us that our inner critic is not the ultimate authority. We have the power to choose which voice we amplify. And what of David, who transformed setbacks into stepping stones? His story underscores that resilience isn't about avoiding falls but rising each time with renewed determination. And let's not forget Maria, who discovered the magic of self-compassion. Her experience teaches us that embracing our imperfections is not a weakness but a powerful act of self-love.

These stories, and the many more that resonate with you, are not mere fables. They are blueprints. They demonstrate the tangible impact of shifting our inner dialogue and consciously choosing affirmations that nurture our growth and fuel our dreams. The power of positive affirmations isn't a magic wand but a consistent practice, a deliberate cultivation of self-belief. As gardeners tend to their plants, we must tend to our minds, weeding out negativity and planting seeds of empowering thoughts.

The journey of personal development is not a destination but a continuous evolution. There will be moments of doubt when the old narratives try to reclaim their space. In those moments, remember the lessons learned, the stories that inspired you. Revisit the affirmations that resonated most deeply, and let them be your anchor in the storm.

Your greatness is not something to be achieved but something to be unveiled. It's already within you, waiting to be nurtured and expressed. As you step forward from this book, carry with you the tools and the inspiration to continue crafting your own story, a story of courage, resilience, and unwavering belief in the magnificent being you are.

Affirm your greatness. Live your greatness. Share your greatness with the world. The tapestry of your life is waiting to be woven, thread by vibrant thread, into a masterpiece of your design.

Conclusion: Embracing a Life of Positivity and Empowerment

As we conclude this journey through the transformative power of positive affirmations, it's essential to reflect on the profound impact that these simple yet powerful statements can have on every aspect of your life. From career success and financial abundance to health, wellness, and meaningful relationships, affirmations are versatile tools that help you create your desired life.

The Journey of Self-Discovery

Throughout this book, we've explored how affirmations can help you:

- **Boost Confidence**: By reinforcing your belief in your abilities and potential.
- **Enhance Focus**: By keeping your goals at the forefront of your mind.

- **Reduce Stress:** By promoting a positive mindset and reducing negative self-talk.
- **Attract Opportunities:** Cultivating a mindset that attracts new opportunities and opens doors to success.

This journey of self-discovery is ongoing. As you continue to practice affirmations, they will become an integral part of your daily routine, helping you navigate life's challenges with grace and resilience.

The Power of Consistency

The key to harnessing the power of affirmations lies in consistency. By incorporating affirmations into your daily routine, you can create lasting change and build a foundation of positivity and empowerment.

Remember, the more you repeat your affirmations, the more they become ingrained in your subconscious mind, shaping your thoughts, beliefs, and actions.

Embracing a Positive Mindset

A positive mindset is the cornerstone of a fulfilling and empowered life. By focusing on the positive aspects of your life and reinforcing them with affirmations, you can shift your perspective and approach each day with optimism and enthusiasm. This positive mindset will benefit you and inspire and uplift those around you.

Taking Action

While affirmations are powerful, they are most effective when combined with action. As you affirm your greatness, take proactive steps toward your goals.

Whether pursuing a new career opportunity, adopting healthier habits, or nurturing your relationships, let your affirmations guide and motivate you to take meaningful action.

Your Path to Empowerment

Embracing a life of positivity and empowerment is a continuous journey. As you move forward, remember to:

- **Stay Committed:** Keep practicing your affirmations daily.
- **Be Patient:** Change takes time, so be patient with yourself and trust the process.
- **Celebrate Your Progress:** Acknowledge and celebrate your achievements, no matter how small.
- **Stay Open:** Be open to new opportunities and experiences that align with your goals.

These principles can create a rich positivity, fulfillment, and empowerment life. Remember, your thoughts and beliefs can shape your reality. Embrace your greatness and let your affirmations guide you towards a brighter, more empowered future.

Thank you for embarking on this journey with me. This book has provided valuable insights and tools to harness the power of positive affirmations. May you continue to affirm your greatness and live a life of positivity and empowerment.

MORE RESOURCES

Check our website: www.dennismotivates.com

YouTube:
https://www.youtube.com/@DennisMbogori

Facebook:
https://www.facebook.com/dennismotivates/

Instagram:
https://www.instagram.com/dennismotivates/

Amazon.com:
https://www.amazon.com/author/dennismbogori